The Art of Baking

The Art of Baking

Mira Thornfield

CONTENTS

Editorial Review	1
Introduction	2
1	Baking Essentials	4
2	The Science Behind Baking	8
3	Breads	12
4	Pastries and Pies	15
5	Cakes and Cupcakes	18
6	Cookies and Bars	22
7	Desserts and Sweet Treats	26
8	Gluten-Free Baking	30
9	Artistic Presentation	34
10	Baking for Special Diets	37
11	Baking for All Occasions	40
12	Baking Tips and Tricks	43
13	Baking Around the World	46
14	Baking as a Business	49
15	Baking with Kids	52

| IV | –

| Conclusion 55

Copyright © 2025 by Mira Thornfield
All rights reserved. No part of this book may be reproduced in any manner whatsoever without written permission except in the case of brief quotations embodied in critical articles and reviews.
First Printing, 2025

Editorial Review

Mira Thornfield's *The Art of Baking: From Pastries to Bread* is a true masterpiece for anyone passionate about baking. This book is more than just a collection of recipes—it's a comprehensive journey through the culture, science, and artistry of baking. Mira's clear, engaging writing style makes even the most complex techniques approachable, and her warmth shines through every page.

Each chapter offers something new to savor, whether you're learning to adapt recipes for gluten-free diets, crafting show-stopping celebration cakes, or teaching the joy of baking to children. The thoughtful inclusion of baking traditions from around the world adds depth and inspiration, making this book a treasure trove of ideas.

Mira's tips and tricks, paired with her approachable explanations, transform baking into an accessible art form for readers of all skill levels. The step-by-step guidance, paired with creative insights, ensures consistently rewarding results. This book is not just a guide—it's a companion for every baker, empowering them to experiment, share, and create.

An absolute must-read for anyone with a love for the kitchen, *The Art of Baking: From Pastries to Bread* is destined to become a timeless classic in the culinary world. Highly recommended!

Introduction

Baking is more than a culinary craft; it is a symphony for the senses and a balm for the soul. The aroma of bread rising in a warm kitchen, the first velvety bite into a perfectly soft cupcake, or the gentle, perfumed essence of rose-flavored shortbread—all these moments evoke comfort, creativity, and connection. Home baking nourishes more than just the body; it fosters a meditative calm, soothing everyday anxieties and offering a profound sense of accomplishment. Beyond that, it is an act of love—one that brings family and friends closer, one batch of cookies or a rustic loaf at a time.

Across the spectrum of baked delights—cakes, tarts, pastries, pizzas, cookies, and bread—there is a humble yet indispensable common denominator: flour. From this essential ingredient comes endless culinary possibilities and memories that linger in every taste.

Imagine filling your home this weekend with the intoxicating fragrance of rose-infused shortbread cookies. These delicate, buttery biscuits are perfect for pairing with a demitasse of espresso or a steaming cup of Earl Grey tea. They're not just a treat for the palate but also an olfactory celebration, as the delicate rose scent weaves through the air. Stored in an airtight container, they'll keep for days (assuming they last that long!), becoming a cherished indulgence for those quiet, contemplative moments or shared company.

The past years have shown us the power of baking to rekindle joy, especially during moments of uncertainty. While there may have been pauses in our routines during lockdowns like Level 3, those were also times when many rediscovered the heartwarming satisfaction of baking at home. Sure, buying a loaf of bread from the supermarket is convenient, but pulling a warm, crackling loaf from your oven—and breaking into it while it's still fresh—is an unparalleled sensory experience. It's a reminder of life's simpler joys and the magic of creating something with your own hands.

This particular recipe was inspired by the blooming roses in my garden during that reflective period. Those vibrant blossoms carried a sensory invitation to experiment, ultimately leading to these simple yet enchanting rose-flavored shortbread cookies. With every nibble, the scent of roses transports me back to moments of calm and creativity.

Ready to be inspired? At the end of the recipe, you'll find suggestions for even more rose-flavored baking adventures. Let's bring a little floral magic into your kitchen.

1

Baking Essentials

Flour: The Journey from Grain to Pantry

The story of flour begins in golden fields of grain, often wheat, though many flours today are a blend of various grains. After the seeds are sown and the wheat ripens to a warm gold, it is harvested and separated from its husks. The process continues with cleaning, often using organic methods to ensure purity. Next, gluten is developed—a step done by hand or machine—followed by sieving, grinding, and conditioning to achieve the ideal texture and protein content. Finally, the flour is bolted to remove any coarse particles and then packed for distribution. What arrives in your pantry is the culmination of this intricate process, ready to transform into delicious creations.

Much like using high-quality cheese, meat, and produce, selecting the right flour is paramount to the success of your baked goods. Not only does it affect flavor, but it also profoundly influences texture. For instance:

- **All-purpose flour**: With its medium protein content, it is a versatile choice for a range of recipes, yielding tender and delicate textures with minimal gluten.

- **Bread flour**: Higher in protein and gluten, it gives dough its structure, producing chewy loaves with a sturdy crumb that holds up to fillings.
- **Pastry flour**: The softest of the trio, it boasts a low protein content, making it the ideal choice for flaky pastries, pies, and delicate baked goods.

Understanding the unique properties of each type of flour ensures your baguettes rise beautifully, your pizza crusts achieve a perfect balance of chewiness, and your cookies maintain their melt-in-your-mouth consistency.

Key Ingredients for Bread Baking

The foundation of bread lies in its ingredients, each contributing to the symphony of flavors and textures. Flour, yeast, water, salt, and sugar are the essential building blocks, but a world of creativity can follow:

- **Flour**: Rich in starch, proteins, and minerals, wheat flour contains gluten—a protein network that traps fermentation gases, allowing dough to rise. Variations include:
  - **Soft wheat flours**: Refined and light, ideal for white bread.
  - **Durum wheat flour**: Protein-rich with a golden hue, used for hearty, shock-resistant breads.
  - **Whole grain or palm flour**: Milled from the seed's outer layer, packed with nutrients.
- **Enhancers**: Professional bakers often incorporate ascorbic acid for improved texture and rise.
- **Extras for creativity**: Milk, eggs, cheeses, chocolates, fruits, and even savory additions like garlic, olives, or seeds.

Each ingredient opens the door to countless possibilities, making bread baking both an art and a science.

Essential Tools and Equipment

The right tools can elevate your baking experience. Here are the must-haves:

- **Mixing Bowls**: Choose durable materials like stainless steel or glass for better visibility and stability. Chilling bowls before whipping egg whites ensures optimal foaming. Rounded Norfolk bowls are versatile, while square ones add a modern twist.
- **Measuring Tools**: Accuracy is key. Use dry cups for solid ingredients, liquid cups for wet ones, and always level measurements for consistency. Sticky ingredients like molasses are best handled in liquid measuring cups.
- **Scales**: Precision scales are indispensable, especially for professional baking. Options range from compact digital models for small batches to traditional platform balances for heavier loads. Choose scales that accommodate both Imperial and metric units for versatility.

Mastering Measurement Techniques

Measurement techniques have evolved significantly over time, from simple ladles for liquid additions to sophisticated digital scales. In modern kitchens:

- Digital scales streamline the process with pre-programmed settings, ensuring accuracy.
- Traditional methods like hand-scooping water into dough continue to charm artisan bakers.

- For smaller items like nuts or cherries, volume measurement by cups still holds its place.

Understanding these techniques ensures every batch is consistent and perfectly executed.

2

The Science Behind Baking

Baking is both an art and a precise science. Each recipe contains a mix of ingredients that, when combined and subjected to heat, undergo a series of chemical reactions to produce a finished product with specific characteristics. Think of it as edible chemistry! For instance, a basic muffin recipe may call for flour, sugar, shortening, egg, milk, baking powder, and salt. Once the batter is placed in a preheated oven, the heat triggers a cascade of chemical transformations. These reactions give rise to the delightful aroma, texture, taste, and color we associate with baked goods.

Take the humble muffin, for example. The goal is to create a product that is light, fluffy, and moist, with a creamy, delicate flavor. Achieving this outcome depends on a precise balance between the ingredients—flour, a leavening agent, liquid, and the proper development of gluten. Eggs, in particular, play a vital role, contributing moisture, protein, and fat while stabilizing the batter through emulsification. This process prevents the fats from bonding chemically, ensuring a uniform texture.

Baking requires accuracy—improvisation like "a pinch of this" or "a spoonful of that" can throw the formula off balance, leading to inconsistent results. By thinking of each recipe as a scientific formula, bakers can ensure success and consistent outcomes by following measurements and procedures precisely.

Leavening Agents: The Rise of Baking

Leavening agents are the heroes behind the rise, volume, and texture of baked goods, introducing air or gas into the dough or batter. Let's explore the key players:

- **Sourdough**: A wild yeast mixture with a distinct, slightly tangy flavor. Although its leavening power is milder than fresh yeast or baking powder, sourdough creates exceptional texture and volume in bread like Pão Carcaça. Its natural fermentation also adds depth to the flavor.
- **Baking Powder**: Unlike yeast, baking powder doesn't require prior activation. When mixed with liquid, it reacts with the acid present to release carbon dioxide, creating a fine, tender crumb. It's commonly used in quick breads and cookies.
- **Yeast**: A classic leavening agent, yeast feeds on sugar and thrives in warm environments, releasing carbon dioxide as it ferments. This not only gives bread its rise but also infuses it with that irresistible aroma. Yeast comes in two main varieties:
    - **Active Dry Yeast**: Requires rehydration in warm water and sugar before use.
    - **Fresh Yeast**: Can be directly mixed with other ingredients.

Beyond these, bakers can explore other leavening agents to achieve unique flavors, textures, and rises in their creations.

Gluten Formation: Building the Structure

The formation of gluten is a critical process in baking. Gluten provides the structure that allows dough to rise and hold its shape. Here's how the magic happens:

1. **Hydration**: When water is added to flour, it begins to penetrate the starch granules, unraveling them and hydrating the proteins—glutenin and gliadin. This slow process allows these proteins to become mobile and start forming bonds.
2. **Kneading**: Mixing or kneading the dough brings these hydrated proteins into contact, allowing them to bond and form a flexible gluten network. As the dough is worked, the matrix becomes stronger, giving the dough elasticity and strength.
3. **Aeration**: Kneading also incorporates air into the dough, stretching the gluten structure further. Dry glutenin connections form, enhancing the dough's ability to hold its shape and support a light, airy texture.

In essence, gluten development transforms a simple flour-water mixture into a cohesive, elastic dough that can trap gases and expand during baking.

Maillard Reaction: The Alchemy of Flavor and Aroma

The Maillard reaction is the secret behind the golden crusts and rich, complex flavors of baked goods. This chemical reaction occurs when proteins and sugars are heated, creating a cascade of new molecules that give baked goods their distinctive aromas and colors.

- **Flavor Compounds**: During the Maillard reaction, molecules like phenols, lactones, and furans are formed. Phenols contribute aromatic complexity, while lactones add ripe, fermented, or tangy notes. Vanillin—a key molecule—produces the delightful, sweet aroma of a crust, reminiscent of vanilla.
- **Aroma Molecules**: Almost no aroma compounds are created in simple sugar-water solutions. However, as sugar is heated, its molecules break apart and recombine into a symphony

of aroma molecules, forming the characteristic smells of caramelization and browning.
- **Visual Appeal**: Beyond flavor, browning also enhances the visual allure of baked goods, making them appear more appetizing.

Understanding the Maillard reaction allows bakers to tweak recipes and ingredients to optimize flavor complexity, from nutty undertones to caramel sweetness.

3

Breads

The Art of Bread Baking

Bread baking is a blend of craft and science, requiring a precise balance of technique, temperature, and timing. For dramatic, crusty breads, a hot and humid atmosphere is key. A general oven temperature of **425°F (220°C)** works well for many breads, creating a robust crust, but softer rolls and buns benefit from a slightly lower temperature of **350°F (175°C)** to prevent over-browning.

Creating steam is crucial for developing a hard crust but can be challenging to manage. A simple method involves placing a pan of hot water in the oven as the bread bakes, then removing it partway through. This technique keeps the process enjoyable without adding unnecessary complexity.

For bread dough that is chilled in the refrigerator, it's important to monitor the fermentation process. While the dough will continue to rise, prolonged refrigeration can result in over-fermentation, leading to an overly acidic flavor. Vigorous bakers may enjoy the nuanced flavors long fermentation brings, but for a lighter, milder-tasting loaf, it's best not to store the dough for more than two weeks.

Maximizing Your Results

- **Sugar in Dough**: Breads containing sugar brown more quickly due to caramelization. To avoid burning, reduce the oven temperature and shorten the baking time for sugary loaves, rolls, and buns.
- **Managing Yeast Dough**: The aroma of yeast dough rising is unmistakably delightful. If a warm environment isn't convenient, enclose the dough with dampened kitchen paper and plastic wrap to trap warm, moist air. Rolls can be chilled before or after shaping by placing them on a cold baking tin or stone, which simplifies handling.

Basic Bread Recipes

The following recipes focus on essential techniques for bread making. They serve as an excellent foundation for beginners, allowing for experimentation and creative variation once mastered. These recipes typically utilize commercial yeast, eliminating the need for long fermentation times.

While it may be tempting to use a stand mixer with a dough hook for large batches, mastering hand-kneading techniques is invaluable. Hand kneading provides an intimate understanding of dough consistency and elasticity—crucial for successful baking. However, it is worth noting that hand-kneading can be labor-intensive and messy, especially with sticky doughs.

Specialty Breads

1. **Sourdough Bread** Sourdough involves a complex fermentation process, relying on wild yeasts and lactic acid bacteria. While it requires patience, sourdough produces dough that is easier to digest, with a tangy flavor and characteristic sourness. It's an artisanal favorite for its depth of flavor and slightly chewy texture.

2. **Ciabatta** Known for its chewy crumb and crispy crust, ciabatta is a classic Italian bread. Its high moisture content creates stretchy gluten strands, but achieving this texture requires excellent gluten formation and ample steam. Too little steam may result in a dense crumb and insufficient rise.
3. **Artisan Favorites**
    - **Focaccia**: A light, airy bread with a soft texture and flavorful olive oil infusion. Its loosely structured dough contrasts with the more compact crumb of ciabatta.
    - **Bolillos**: A Mexican roll similar to baguettes but shaped uniquely. Teleras, a close cousin, are more readily available in many regions.
    - **Baguettes**: Perhaps the most challenging to perfect, baguettes require specific equipment and careful technique to achieve their iconic crust and airy interior.

Sourdough Techniques

In traditional yeasted doughs, the Maillard reaction dominates flavor development, creating rich, savory notes. Sourdough introduces another dimension, producing phenols, lactic acids, and ethyl alcohols that contribute to its characteristic tang and complexity.

Creating a sourdough starter begins with equal parts flour and water, left to ferment over several days. Microbial life, including wild yeasts and bacteria, develops naturally. For the modern baker, controlling this environment is key. By feeding the starter with whole-grain flour (low in nutrients), you can encourage specific microbial strains to thrive while suppressing others, much like ancient Han dynasty bakers perfected their methods thousands of years ago.

4

Pastries and Pies

The Legacy of Puff Pastry

Italy proudly claims to be the birthplace of puff pastry, a culinary marvel perfected by skilled hands since the Middle Ages. However, its history is intertwined with the evolution of dough-making across cultures. Phyllo dough, for instance, dates back to Byzantine times, and the Spaniards inherited semi-puff pastry techniques from the Arabs. Over time, puff pastry began to fade in certain regions, overshadowed by other baking traditions.

The modern era introduced a practical solution with frozen pastry sheets—a convenient substitute that allows even amateur bakers to experience the joys of puff pastry without starting from scratch. Many recipes today rely on these ready-made sheets, which bridge the gap between tradition and modern convenience. For now, puff pastry is a freezer staple, perfect for crafting elegant treats when life calls for something truly special.

The Roots of Pastry

Pastry is one of civilization's most delectable contributions, though its origins reveal a history of slow evolution. The Greeks first wrapped meat in leaves and flour paste before baking, while the Romans refined this practice by replacing the leaves with a thin bread crust. They even coined the term **crustum**, which referred to the pastry shell apart from its filling.

A charming legend attributes the invention of puff pastry to an Arab baker named Absalam in the Iberian Peninsula. Frustrated women allegedly threw a bucket of butter and a bag of flour at him, demanding he work faster. The serendipitous mix resulted in one of the Middle Ages' most beloved pastries.

Classic Pastry Dough

Mastering pastry dough is essential for creating tarts, pies, and quiches. Among the classics is **pâte brisée**, a versatile shortcrust dough known for its tender texture and subtle flavor. Success depends on two factors: the type of ingredients and their temperature. Here are some key tips:

1. **Ingredient Choice**: Use all-purpose flour for quick bakes, such as tarts, while spelt flour is better for recipes requiring longer baking times, like quiches.
2. **Butter Quality**: True short pastry demands high-quality butter, ideally slightly stale, for richer flavor. For a lighter version, oil can be used as a substitute.
3. **Flavors**: Customize your dough by incorporating flavors such as lemon zest, rosemary, or Parmigiano-Reggiano cheese for savory options. When making savory pies or quiches, eliminate sugar and add a pinch of salt for balance.

This foundational dough invites endless creativity, offering a canvas for both sweet and savory creations.

Sweet and Savory Fillings

A pastry is defined by its filling, be it sweet or savory. Without a filling, it ceases to be a pastry. The choices are virtually limitless:

- **Sweet**: Think fruit-filled Danish pastries, creamy custard tarts, or croissants layered with chocolate or almond paste.
- **Savory**: Spanakopita, a traditional Greek pastry filled with spinach and feta, or pizzaretas—mini hand pies filled with cheese and vegetables—are delightful options.

The filling's consistency is crucial. Liquid fillings, for example, rely on flour starches to thicken and set during baking, ensuring a perfect balance of moisture and texture. Each pastry requires specific baking temperatures to achieve golden-brown perfection without compromising its interior.

Pie Crust Variations

Pie crusts offer a playground for creativity, from decorative edges pressed with a fork to intricate lattice designs. Here are some tips for success:

- **Resting the Dough**: After mixing, let the dough rest briefly in the refrigerator to relax the gluten. Avoid over-chilling, as it softens quickly during rolling.
- **Fitting the Mold**: Roll the dough out evenly to a thickness of 3–4 mm (1/8 to 3/16 inch). Allow a slight overhang at the edges to create a sturdy wall during baking.
- **Customization**: Add cocoa powder to the flour mixture for a chocolate crust, or sift confectioner's sugar into the dough for a sweeter, more delicate finish. Keep in mind that sweeter doughs are better suited for shorter baking times.

A well-executed crust provides the foundation for garnishes like ganache, cooked creams, or fresh fruit, resulting in a visually striking dessert with exquisite flavor.

5

Cakes and Cupcakes

A **Symbol of Celebration**
"Let them eat cake." A phrase often misattributed to a queen during times of scarcity—it resonates with the idea that cake embodies indulgence, abundance, and joy. Historically, the "cake" they referred to bore little resemblance to the desserts we know today, but the sentiment remains true. Cake is synonymous with celebration. From feast tables to weddings adorned with multi-tiered masterpieces, cakes mark life's milestones with sweetness and artistry.

Cake's origins, like those of friendship, are shrouded in mystery. What we do know is that as long as people have roasted meat over hearth fires, they've also gathered to share some form of baked sweet. Whether a shortbread cookie, a mince pie, or a sticky bun, such offerings have brought loved ones together through the ages. After all, who could decline a slice of cake and still call themselves a friend?

The Evolution of Cake

At their core, cakes and cupcakes might once have been seen as individual loaves of sweetened flatbread. Today, however, we distinguish them from quick breads by their complexity and chemistry. Ancient civilizations likely didn't conceive of "quick bread" as we do, yet they developed countless recipes for sweetened loaves and offerings, blending science and tradition long before modern baking tools and techniques came into play.

Butter Cakes

Butter cakes stand out for their rich flavors and textures. They can be categorized as:

- **Light Butter Cakes**: Require gentle heating during preparation.
- **Dark Butter Cakes**: Omit the heat treatment and emphasize deeper flavors.

A typical butter cake batter involves creaming butter and sugar, then integrating eggs, lemon juice, oil, and other liquids. The dry ingredients—flour and baking powder—are added last, with careful mixing to avoid overworking the batter. Proper technique ensures a soft, fluffy texture, though overbaking can result in drier, less flavorful cakes.

Choosing the right cake tin is essential. Round, straight-edged tins work best, and it's advisable to line the bottom with parchment paper for easy release. Grease the sides with butter or a specialized pan fat to ensure smooth edges.

Sponge Cakes

Sponge cakes are named for their airy, sponge-like texture created by countless air cells. A well-made sponge cake feels light and bouncy to the touch and has a fine, uniform crumb. Achieving this requires careful mixing, which incorporates air into the batter, and precision during baking. Here's a simple recipe to start with:

- **Ingredients**:
    - 4 eggs (separated)
    - 1 cup powdered sugar

- 2 tablespoons cold water
- 1 1/4 cups flour
- 1 teaspoon vanilla extract
- 1 teaspoon lemon extract
- 1/2 teaspoon salt

Steps:

1. Beat egg yolks until thick and light in color, then mix in sugar and water.
2. Sift together flour and salt, then add them to the yolk mixture.
3. Whip egg whites to stiff peaks and gently fold them into the batter.
4. Add flavorings and fold lightly to combine.
5. Pour into a lined 12x8x2-inch baking pan and bake in a moderate oven (around 350°F/175°C) for 20 minutes.
6. Turn out onto a cloth dusted with powdered sugar, and decorate or frost as desired.

This basic sponge cake can be dressed up with fruits, jams, or creative decorations.

Frosting and Decoration

Cakes truly shine when adorned with frosting, fruits, or intricate designs. Almond cream frosting pairs beautifully with fruit-based cakes, while melted jam can provide a shiny glaze or act as an adhesive for nuts and decorations. Here are some tips:

- Use a springform pan lined with parchment for seamless sponge cake preparation.
- Save leftover dough for crafting crumbly biscuits or other small treats.

- Experiment with frostings to complement different cakes, such as almond or buttercream for rich textures or whipped cream for lighter desserts.

Decorating offers endless opportunities to infuse personality and artistry into your cakes. From fruit cut into fancy shapes to delicate piping, the possibilities are as limitless as your imagination.

6

Cookies and Bars

Mastering the Art of Cookie Baking
Cookies are versatile, delightful, and surprisingly easy to bake when armed with the right tools and techniques. Whether you're mixing by hand, using a hand-held mixer, or opting for the convenience of a stand mixer, attention to detail is key. A stand mixer is particularly efficient, cutting down prep time and ensuring a consistent batter.

For perfect results:

- **Creaming Matters**: Start by creaming your butter and shortening ingredients until the mixture is light, fluffy, and pale yellow.
- **Scrape Often**: Keep a spatula handy to scrape down the bowl after every ingredient addition.
- **Mix Mindfully**: Avoid over-mixing. Blend dry and wet ingredients just until incorporated to maintain the dough's integrity.
- **Temperature Awareness**: Ensure all your ingredients are at the recommended temperature, especially soft butter or other shortening ingredients, unless stated otherwise.

- **Flour Precision**: Weighing flour is the most accurate method. If measuring by volume, lightly spoon flour into a measuring cup and level it with a spatula for precision.

Chilling cookie sheets and portioning dough while it's still easy to handle can also help maintain texture and shape. A perfectly baked cookie begins with careful preparation, making these tips indispensable for any baker.

Why Cookies and Bars?

Cookies and bars hold a special place in celebrations, offering sweetness and creativity in equal measure. They're perfect for marking milestones, holidays, or simply sharing joy with others. This chapter offers a treasure trove of recipes, from classic favorites to innovative treats, alongside helpful baking tips and inspiration. Let your oven be the heart of your celebrations!

Classic Cookie Recipes

Cookies come in countless varieties, each with its own story and charm. From golden refrigerator cookies to lacy Florentines, the options are endless. Here's a snapshot of classic recipes:

- **Sugar Cookies**: Versatile and easy to decorate.
- **Oatmeal-Coconut Cookies**: A chewy, tropical twist.
- **Madeleine Cookies**: Delicate French sponge-like delights.
- **Chocolate-Mint Cookies**: A refreshing combination.
- **Brownie-Cheesecake Cookies**: A decadent fusion of two favorites.

Assembling a cookie platter is a creative endeavor—package your creations in a gift box with bright tissue paper for a thoughtful surprise. Whether you're baking for loved ones or indulging your sweet tooth, cookies are a simple yet satisfying treat.

Bar Cookie Varieties

Bar cookies combine the ease of one-pot preparation with the indulgence of layered flavors and textures. Among the standout options are:

- **Brownies**: Rich and fudgy, made with melted chocolate, butter, and sugar.
- **Oatmeal Varieties**: Featuring flavors like walnut, cherry, or caramel.
- **Coconut Mounds**: Snowy bars with a tropical flair.
- **Fruity Bars**: Cherry pie, rhubarb, or citrus-infused delights.
- **Magic Bars**: Endless variations layered with chocolate, nuts, and condensed milk.

Bars often use a base mixture, such as melted chocolate or cream cheese, and allow for endless customization with nuts, dried fruits, or flavorings. They're crowd-pleasers for any gathering, delivering big flavor with minimal effort.

Cookie Decorating Techniques

Decoration transforms cookies from simple sweets to edible art. While precision tools like fine watercolor brushes or pastry bags with graduated tips add flair, creativity is the true secret ingredient. Here are some tips:

1. **Custom Icing**: Blend powdered food coloring into royal icing for custom hues like saffron, tangerine, or avocado green.
2. **Layered Textures**: Experiment with shimmering sugar, edible dragees, or finely chopped nuts for visual appeal.
3. **Gilded Outlines**: Use royal icing to create sharp, defined shapes or elegant borders.

COOKIES AND BARS

Whether it's bright holiday-themed sugar cookies or intricate gingerbread designs, decorating is as much about fun as it is about flavor.

# 7

Desserts and Sweet Treats

Flan Cakes: A Timeless Treat

Flan cakes have long been a hallmark of dessert tables, blending creamy textures with rich flavors. In the absence of soft wheat flour, a mix of hard wheat flour, potato starch, and buckwheat flour serves as an excellent substitute, ensuring a perfectly tender outcome. These cakes use fewer eggs and rely on a precise method of preparation:

- Combine the ingredients over low heat, stirring continuously with a wooden spoon.
- Gradually incorporate warmed liquid, such as rosé, into the batter, raising the heat in stages.
- Alternate between stirring and heating to achieve a smooth, consistent mixture.
- Once cooled, the flan is poured into a prepared cake crust, ready to be garnished with vanilla or chocolate.

Historically, flan cakes have been a versatile and adaptable dessert, cherished across cultures for their simplicity and elegance.

The Heritage of Fritters, Crêpes, and Waffles

Long before the rise of pastry shops, fritter vendors dominated morning markets, supplying warm, crispy delights to eager crowds. These enterprising bakers carried a small stove, or *hotte*, which they used to heat oil and cook their offerings. Fritters, crêpes, and waffles remain beloved staples, blending history with irresistible flavors. Whether enjoyed fresh from the vendor or prepared at home, they encapsulate the joy of traditional treats.

Puddings and Custards

Bread Pudding: A Southern Comfort

Bread puddings are both economical and endlessly customizable, offering a canvas for creativity. Made with basic custard and leftover bread, they can be elevated with additions such as:

- **Dried Fruits**: Raisins, cherries, apricots, or cranberries.
- **Nuts and Berries**: For added texture and flavor.
- **Toppings**: Pair with hard sauce (a sweet blend of butter, sugar, vanilla, and bourbon) or whipped cream flavored with brandy.

Two main styles exist:

1. **Traditional Bread Pudding**: Chewy and doughy, made with stale bread soaked in sugar and milk.
2. **Cake-like Bread Pudding**: A fluffier version popular in modern restaurants, achieved by thoroughly saturating the bread and allowing it to rest before baking.

Both styles highlight the versatility of this classic dessert, ensuring it remains a favorite for generations.

Fruit Desserts

Tarts: A Dainty Delight

Tarts are a celebration of both flavor and presentation, with their open, fluted crusts and vibrant fillings. In contrast to pies, which feature a fully enclosed filling, tarts emphasize visual and culinary artistry. Key tips for tart-making include:

- Experimenting with shapes and sizes, from single-serving portions to grand multi-portion displays.
- Exploring a variety of fillings, such as custards, fresh fruits, or jams.
- Enhancing the appeal with garnishes like edible flowers, powdered sugar, or candied fruits.

Perfect for high tea or celebratory events, tarts are an elegant addition to any dessert spread.

Chocolate Delights

The Timeless Allure of Chocolate

Few ingredients evoke passion like chocolate. Once reserved for the elite, chocolate has evolved into a universal symbol of indulgence. It holds the power to transform moods, lifting spirits with its rich, velvety allure. Genuine chocolate—free from artificial additives—offers unparalleled depth and complexity, whether in petit fours, éclairs, or classic chocolate cakes.

A Love Affair with Chocolate:

- Chocolate connects generations, from old-fashioned petit fours to modern innovations.
- Its versatility shines in desserts, from molten lava cakes to handcrafted truffles.
- For chocoholics, a single bite holds the magic to brighten even the cloudiest day.

DESSERTS AND SWEET TREATS

To truly appreciate chocolate, one must savor it in its purest form—unadulterated and unapologetically indulgent.

8

Gluten-Free Baking

The Basics of Gluten-Free Baking

Embarking on the journey of gluten-free baking can be both exciting and rewarding. With a bit of research and experimentation, you can transform your favorite recipes into gluten-free masterpieces. Start by replacing regular flour with gluten-free flour blends and incorporating a binding agent like xanthan gum, which mimics the elasticity of gluten. For those avoiding xanthan gum, alternative binders such as chia seeds, psyllium husk, or flaxseed can work just as effectively.

Here are some essential tips to perfect your gluten-free bakes:

- **Blend Your Flours**: A combination of gluten-free flours (e.g., rice, almond, and tapioca) offers a balanced texture and flavor.
- **Adjust Hydration**: Gluten-free flours are often denser and more absorbent. Add wet ingredients gradually and let the batter sit to allow the flour to hydrate fully.
- **Avoid Over-Mixing**: Overworking the batter can lead to tough, dry baked goods.
- **Use Wet Ingredients**: Juicy fruits or vegetables, like apples or zucchini, can enhance moisture in cakes and breads.

Remember, gluten-free baking requires patience and persistence, but the results can be just as delicious as their gluten-based counterparts.

Why Choose Gluten-Free?

Gluten-free diets are essential for those with celiac disease, an autoimmune condition triggered by gluten—a protein found in wheat, rye, and barley. Beyond medical necessity, many people reduce gluten for health or dietary reasons. Eliminating gluten doesn't mean sacrificing flavor or texture; it simply calls for adapting recipes and exploring new ingredients.

Alternative Flours

The wide range of gluten-free flours offers exciting possibilities, though each has unique characteristics:

- **Quinoa Flour**: High in protein with a strong, nutty flavor. Works well in dense baked goods but may result in a drier texture.
- **Rice Flour**: Versatile and neutral in flavor, perfect for blending.
- **Chickpea Flour**: Adds a subtle earthiness and is great for savory bakes.
- **Almond Flour**: Moist and mildly sweet, ideal for cookies and cakes.
- **Sorghum Flour**: Adds structure and pairs well with starches like tapioca or potato.

Experimentation is key, as no single gluten-free flour can directly replace wheat flour. Combining flours often yields the best results, balancing flavor, texture, and moisture.

Substitutions and Modifications

Baking substitutions can be a lifesaver when specific ingredients aren't available. Here are some handy swaps:

- **Vinegar**: Replace 1 tablespoon of wine vinegar with apple cider or distilled vinegar for equivalent acidity.
- **Buttermilk**: Combine 1 cup of milk with 1 tablespoon of vinegar, or use plain yogurt as a substitute.
- **Sugar Alternatives**: Use 2/3 cup honey or 3/4 cup maple syrup for every cup of sugar, reducing liquid in the recipe by 1/4 cup.

Feel free to experiment, but keep in mind that precision is critical in gluten-free baking, unlike the freer nature of cooking.

Tips for Gluten-Free Recipes

Renowned gluten-free baker Linda Engdahl suggests using milk—be it fresh, reconstituted dry milk, or non-dairy substitutes—as a liquid base for gluten-free recipes. Milk helps achieve a good rise and oven spring. Additionally:

- **Xanthan Gum**: Just 1/2 teaspoon per cup of flour adds structure to breads and pastries.
- **Pie Crusts**: Blending rice and corn flour creates tender, flaky crusts.
- **Yorkshire Puddings**: Sorghum flour mixes or 20% corn flour substitutions produce delightful "Yorkshire Crunchies."

Playing with flour combinations is the secret to creating diverse gluten-free baked goods, from pastries to bread.

Flexible Gluten-Free Flour Mix

Creating your own gluten-free flour mix allows for customization and cost-effectiveness:

- Combine several flours (e.g., rice, almond, and sorghum) with starches like tapioca or potato starch.
- Mix in xanthan gum to ensure an even distribution for consistent results.
- Proof yeast using 1 teaspoon of sugar instead of the usual tablespoon to adapt the recipe for gluten-free dough.

This approach ensures you'll always have a versatile mix on hand for various recipes.

9
Artistic Presentation

The Aesthetic Appeal

Presentation is just as important as flavor when it comes to baked goods. The visual harmony of colors, shapes, and textures must be thoughtfully considered alongside the chosen setting—a tray, placemat, basket, or base that complements the baked product. Together, these elements transform a pastry or loaf into an artistic centerpiece, drawing eyes and sparking appetites. Skilled bakers and pastry chefs know that a thoughtfully framed product stands out, creating not only an enticing treat but also a memorable experience.

From fresh herb sprigs like basil, parsley, or dill to vibrant edible flowers such as viola or nasturtium, embellishments enhance the natural beauty of baked goods. Even a simple addition, such as a scattering of powdered sugar or a drizzle of glaze, can create a stunning effect.

Plating Techniques
The Art of Composition

Plating is a vital step in dessert presentation, capturing attention and conveying creativity. While main courses often feature multiple components presented in a flat space, desserts should evoke a sense of elegance and elevation. Roundness and volume are hallmarks of dessert plating, and the use of low bowls or dishes emphasizes these qualities beautifully.

Here are some essentials for plating desserts:

1. **Focus on Volume**: Layer components to add height and dimension.
2. **Create a Focal Point**: Allow the dessert to stand out as the star of the plate, surrounded by complementary garnishes.
3. **Balance Colors and Textures**: Contrasting elements—such as a crisp wafer alongside a creamy mousse—enhance visual and sensory appeal.

Desserts are often the grand finale of a meal, and their presentation should reflect this, leaving diners with a lasting impression of artistry and indulgence.

Garnishing and Decoration
Harmonious Embellishments
Decorating baked goods is a delightful way to enhance both flavor and appearance. From classic options like buttercream and fondant to more creative garnishes, the possibilities are endless:

- **Edible Decorations**: Use fresh fruits, herbs, nuts, or flowers for natural beauty.
- **Textural Contrast**: Add chopped nuts, cocoa powder, or chocolate shavings for a sophisticated touch.
- **Fondant and Buttercream**: These versatile materials allow for intricate designs, from flowers to figurines.

For fruits prone to browning, such as apples or bananas, a splash of lemon juice can preserve their color. Balancing aesthetics with functionality ensures that decorations feel natural and appealing rather than overly contrived.

Food Photography Tips
Capturing Culinary Masterpieces

A picture is worth a thousand bites, and great food photography can make your baked goods irresistible. To achieve stunning results:

- **Focus on Details**: Highlight the textures, colors, and unique features of your baked creation. A close-up of a flaky crust or a perfectly swirled frosting can tell a story.
- **Experiment with Angles**: Play with perspective to guide the viewer's eye. Overhead shots work well for symmetrical designs, while angled views add depth.
- **Master the Lighting**: Soft, diffused light creates the most flattering images. Take advantage of natural light near windows or shoot outdoors during the golden hours (morning or evening).

Preparation is key—style your shot before snapping the photo. A half-sliced bread loaf, a drizzle of chocolate, or a dusting of powdered sugar can evoke emotion and inspire your audience to recreate your recipe.

10

Baking for Special Diets

Accommodating Dietary Needs
Baking can be adapted to suit a variety of dietary requirements without compromising flavor or quality. By understanding ingredient properties and making thoughtful substitutions, you can create treats that cater to gluten-free, vegan, paleo, low-sugar, or calorie-conscious diets. Whether modifying recipes for personal health or for loved ones, inclusive baking begins with creativity and the willingness to experiment.

Gluten-Free Baking
For those with gluten intolerance or celiac disease, gluten-free baking opens a world of possibilities:

- **Flour Blends**: Use a combination of gluten-free flours like rice, almond, or chickpea to balance texture and flavor.
- **Binding Agents**: Xanthan gum, psyllium husk, or ground flaxseed mimic the elasticity of gluten, creating structure in baked goods.
- **Adaptation Tips**:
    - Combine heavier flours like oat or rye with lighter ones to avoid dense textures.

- Allow batter to rest before baking to let the flours hydrate fully.
- For bread, focus on creating a strong dough structure by mixing flours until the desired consistency is achieved.

Gluten-free recipes can be surprisingly versatile. Breads like babka, cinnamon swirl, or chocolate rolls—and even desserts like peach melba and almond cream strudels—can be tailored to this diet with the right flour substitutions and techniques.

Vegan Baking

Baking without eggs or dairy is not only achievable but also delicious. Vegan baking often relies on creative substitutes:

- **Egg Replacers**:
  1. Mix 1 tablespoon of ground flaxseed with 2.5 tablespoons of water for muffins or cookies.
  2. Use 2 tablespoons of applesauce or a quarter of a mashed banana for moist cakes.
  3. Blend silken tofu or oatmeal for softer bread textures.

Vegan baking also focuses on unrefined sweeteners like maple syrup or agave nectar and plant-based milks such as almond, oat, or coconut milk. While traditional eggs add structure and moisture, vegan alternatives ensure the same results with a fresh twist on flavor.

Paleo-Friendly Baking

Paleo baking celebrates natural, minimally processed ingredients, catering to those sensitive to gluten or grains:

- **Flour Substitutes**: Ground nuts and seeds, such as almond or coconut flour, replace traditional flours.

- **Natural Sweeteners**: Swap sugar for honey, maple syrup, or dates to maintain a paleo-friendly approach.
- **Tips for Success**:
  - Use green banana flour for its high resistant starch, but ensure proper baking to avoid a damp texture.
  - Add nuts and seeds for flavor and nutritional benefits.

Paleo baked goods often freeze well, making meal prep convenient. Remember, baking times may vary with alternative flours—test for doneness before removing items from the oven.

Low-Sugar and Diabetic-Friendly Baking

For those reducing sugar or managing diabetes, thoughtful substitutions can create indulgent yet health-conscious treats:

- **Sweeteners**: Use polyols like maltitol or natural options like stevia. Maltitol has 75-90% of the sweetness of sugar but doesn't crystallize, making it ideal for pastries.
- **Bulking Agents**: Combine sweeteners in proper proportions to ensure pastries rise correctly and maintain their structure.
- **Key Tips**:
  - Low-sugar recipes require careful adjustments to leavening agents.
  - Expect subtle flavor differences compared to traditional sugar-based recipes.

These techniques allow bakers to craft diabetic-friendly desserts, from cakes to cookies, without sacrificing taste or texture.

11

Baking for All Occasions

Birthday Cakes: The Heart of the Celebration
No birthday is complete without a cake, the centerpiece of festive traditions. Everyone eagerly awaits the singing of "Happy Birthday," the joyous ritual of blowing out candles, and the grand moment of cutting the cake—a symbol of shared happiness. Cakes have transformed over generations to reflect personality and creativity, coming in every imaginable shape, size, and flavor.

Among the favorites:

- **Fairy Cakes**: Simple and versatile, they are beloved by all ages and perfect for spontaneous cravings or thoughtful gifting. These single-serving treats are as delightful to make as they are to enjoy.
- **Chocolate Cakes and Brownies**: Rich and decadent, they are staples for larger parties, with "Chocolate Fingers" being a whimsical and nostalgic favorite.
- **Muffins and Fruited Scones**: While muffins hold a modest spot, fruited scones win approval as part of a luxurious afternoon tea, especially when paired with clotted cream and homemade jam.

From modest fairy cakes to towering birthday confections, cakes remain at the heart of every celebration, infusing moments with sweetness and joy.

Holiday Baking: Warmth and Tradition

The holidays bring families together, and nothing creates a festive atmosphere quite like the aroma of baked goods wafting through the air. Yeasted breads and buns are cherished staples at these gatherings, offering both tradition and a touch of fun:

- **Easter Treats**: Try shaping buns and placing a colorful plastic egg inside each one, tied with a ribbon. The ribbon changes color during baking, adding a playful element to the table. Guests can remove the egg and enjoy a delicious surprise filling like chicken salad.
- **Advance Preparation**: For time-saving solutions, prepare your dough in advance using a "Basic Master Dough" recipe. Store it in the refrigerator for up to ten days and bake fresh rolls or breads as needed.

Whether it's sweet loaves for Christmas morning or savory buns for a family dinner, holiday baking celebrates connection and togetherness.

Celebration Cakes

Birthday Cakes

Personalizing birthday cakes adds a magical touch to any celebration. A simple yet charming idea is to create a custom birthday banner:

1. **Materials Needed**: Paper, toothpicks, skewers, glue, and scissors.

2. **How-To**: Cut out paper letters or flags, glue them to toothpicks, and string them along a skewer as bunting. Place the skewer into the center of the cake.
3. **Add Fun**: Inflate a balloon and secure it to the cake for a festive surprise. After singing and celebrating, be sure to remove the balloon before cutting.

Celebrating milestones with unique decorations and themes ensures each birthday feels extra special.

Wedding Cakes

Wedding cakes have evolved into expressions of individuality, showcasing the couple's style and story. Options are endless:

- **Flavors and Frostings**: From traditional vanilla sponge to bold chocolate ganache, flavors are tailored to the couple's tastes. Frosting choices include fondant, buttercream, or marzipan.
- **Creative Touches**: Modern cakes often feature monograms, sugar flowers, or designs inspired by shared hobbies.
- **Seamless Finish**: Applying food-safe acetate before decorating ensures smooth, professional edges for a flawless presentation.

Once a symbol of fertility, the wedding cake has transformed into a token of shared joy, with the cutting ceremony now a cherished moment captured in photographs.

12

Baking Tips and Tricks

Efficiency in Preparation
Success in baking begins with proper preparation:

- **Room Temperature Ingredients**: Ingredients like eggs, butter, and dairy mix more smoothly and evenly when at room temperature. To speed up the process:
    - Place eggs in a bowl of lukewarm water for 10 minutes.
    - Remove dairy from the fridge before you start measuring the remaining ingredients, allowing them to warm up naturally.
- **Accurate Measuring**:
    - Use dry measuring cups for solids like flour and sugar. Level off dry ingredients with a knife for precision.
    - Use liquid measuring cups for wet ingredients. Pour to the appropriate line and check at eye level to ensure accuracy. Avoid using measuring cups or spoons as scoops, which can lead to inconsistent measurements.

By prioritizing these small steps, you'll ensure consistent results every time.

Troubleshooting Common Baking Issues

Overcome challenges with these tried-and-true solutions:

- **Browning Too Quickly**: Tent a piece of aluminum foil over the top of your baked goods to prevent over-browning while allowing the interior to cook through.
- **Moisture Retention**: Place a shallow pan of hot water in the oven to create steam. This technique is especially effective for whole-grain breads, enhancing crust browning and texture.
- **Uneven Browning**: Halfway through baking, swap the positions of pans on different racks to ensure even heat distribution.
- **Odor Transfer**: Avoid baking aromatic goods like cinnamon buns in the same oven used for strong-smelling foods. Use deodorized or unscented flour to maintain purity in flavor.

These tips help address common pitfalls and elevate your baked goods' quality.

Time-Saving Techniques

In today's fast-paced world, efficiency matters:

- **Pre-Cut Ingredients**: Dice butter and chill it while preparing other ingredients. This keeps the fat cold, resulting in flakier pastries.
- **Mix Smartly**: Use a food processor with a steel blade to pulse fat into flour until the mixture resembles coarse crumbs.
- **Simplify Dough Handling**: Instead of rolling, pat out biscuit or pie dough inside a resealable plastic bag for hassle-free shaping.
- **Egg Substitutes for Tenderness**: A tablespoon of egg substitute can replicate the fat in yolks, reducing gluten development while enhancing tenderness.

These techniques save time without sacrificing flavor or texture, making baking approachable for everyone.

Flavor Enhancements

Take your baked goods to the next level with these creative ideas:

- **Fruits**: Thinly sliced apples add moisture and sweetness to bread. Orange zest creates an aromatic, citrusy twist perfect for raisin or cranberry bread.
- **Whole Grains**: Dust semolina under your loaf for crunch and nutty flavor. Using whole grains or unbleached flours enhances flavor while providing essential nutrients.
- **Herbs**: Infuse bread with rosemary, oregano, or marjoram for a savory touch. Focaccia bread, for instance, comes alive with a drizzle of olive oil and a sprinkle of rosemary.
- **Seeds**: Poppy seeds, aniseed, or sunflower seeds not only elevate flavor but also boost nutritional content. For example, rye bread's characteristic taste often comes from caraway seeds.

The possibilities are endless—flavor combinations are limited only by your imagination.

13

Baking Around the World

Mexican Traditions
In Mexico, tortillas—crafted from either flour or corn—are a cornerstone of every meal. From breakfast to dinner, they serve as a versatile base for countless dishes, embodying simplicity and tradition. Flour tortillas, in particular, are popular for wrapping stews or sautéed vegetables, while corn tortillas shine in tacos, enchiladas, and tostadas. Mexican baking extends to celebratory breads like **Pan de Muerto**, a sweet bread adorned with bone-like decorations, and **Rosca de Reyes**, a fruit-studded bread enjoyed during the Epiphany.

Nepal and South Asia
Nepalese cuisine offers an extraordinary variety of bread, often made with barley, wheat, or rice flour. Barley bread, paired with vegetables or lentils, reflects the vegan influences prevalent in the region. The Nepalese kitchen is alive with herbs and spices, transforming simple ingredients into dishes rich in flavor and aroma. Neighboring South Asia celebrates breads like **chapati**, **naan**, and **roti**, integral to daily meals and made from wheat flour. In Rajasthan, India, bread is a lifeline for travelers, paired simply with salt for sustenance.

West African Staples

Across West Africa, **fufu** serves as a staple food with endless variations. Made from cassava, yam, plantain, or rice, its soft, spongy texture pairs perfectly with hearty stews. This humble dough sustains families and communities, reflecting the ingenuity of African cuisine. In South Africa, bread-making takes many forms, from the steamed dumplings of Xhosa culture to the iconic **potbrood** baked over open flames.

French Elegance

France is synonymous with bread, from the iconic baguette to rustic **pain de campagne**. Traditional French baking relies on slow fermentation and high hydration doughs, resulting in unparalleled textures and flavors. Parisian boulangeries showcase the artistry of French bakers, where laminated croissants and brioches line the shelves. French bread has become a global benchmark, a testament to its enduring influence.

Italian Heritage

Italy boasts over 350 types of bread, each reflecting regional diversity. In **Puglia**, the agricultural heart of Italy, bread-making traditions like **Puccia** reign supreme. This soft, stuffed bread is celebrated during festivals, symbolizing the deep connection between food and culture. From the **ciabatta** of the north to the **pane sciocco** of Tuscany, Italian breads are a reflection of the country's culinary soul, often enjoyed with olive oil, cheeses, and cured meats.

Asian Baking Traditions

Asia's baking culture spans centuries, blending innovation with tradition:

- **China**: Steamed bread, such as barbecue pork buns (**cha siu bao**), showcases the fusion of herbal and savory flavors. The delicate artistry of Chinese bakers continues to inspire.

- **Japan**: Japanese bakeries fuse European techniques with local ingredients, offering creations like soft milk bread (**shokupan**) and sweet melon pan. These bakeries have become hubs of innovation, where technology meets culinary precision.

Baking as a Universal Language

From the flatbreads of India to the festive breads of Mexico, baking unites cultures through shared traditions. It's not just about nourishment—it's about storytelling, connection, and celebrating the universal comfort of bread.

14

Baking as a Business

The Evolution of Baking

Bread, a timeless commodity, symbolizes more than sustenance—it tells the story of humanity's cultural and culinary evolution. Baking, whether for pleasure or business, is both a therapeutic process and an art. The simple act of crafting a loaf of bread, or a beautifully iced cake, is rooted in history while offering an outlet for creativity and connection. Bread and cakes, despite their science-driven precision, also thrive on artistic expression, uniting modern techniques with age-old traditions.

The allure of baking lies not only in its ability to nourish the body but also in its capacity to feed the soul, build communities, and inspire gratitude—essential qualities when turning this passion into a business.

Starting a Home Bakery
Step One: Planning and Research

Launching a home bakery requires careful thought:

- **Business Plan**: Develop a written plan outlining your goals, target audience, pricing strategy, and recipes. This not only organizes your ideas but also demonstrates professionalism when approaching banks or lenders.

- **Regulations**: Research local and state food laws to ensure compliance. Home bakeries often have specific requirements regarding permits, labeling, and hygiene.
- **Initial Investment**: With a well-equipped kitchen, you can start with as little as $500. Essentials like three baking pans, $50 in supplies, and personal dedication can lay the foundation for success.

A home bakery offers an accessible and affordable pathway to turn your baking hobby into a viable business. Whether selling at craft fairs or filling custom orders, this venture allows you to start small while dreaming big.

Marketing and Branding
Building Your Brand

The individuality of artisanal baking shines in a competitive market. Distinguish your bakery by telling its story—what inspired you, what sets your products apart, and why customers should choose you:

- **Leverage Digital Marketing**: Build a professional website showcasing your baked goods. Use social media platforms to share visuals, engage with customers, and announce specials or seasonal products.
- **Celebrate Authenticity**: Consumers value handmade, quality-focused products. Highlight unique selling points, such as locally sourced ingredients, gluten-free options, or family recipes.

While word-of-mouth remains powerful, today's bakeries thrive by combining traditional methods with modern marketing tools, ensuring their stories and offerings reach the widest audience.

Pricing and Profitability
The Art of Pricing

Pricing is one of the most challenging aspects of running a bakery. Follow these steps to strike a balance:

1. **Calculate Costs**:
   - **Direct Costs**: Ingredients and packaging.
   - **Indirect Costs**: Gas, electricity, water, insurance, and hygiene practices.
2. **Understand Your Market**:
   - Research competitors and analyze their pricing.
   - Emphasize your bakery's strengths, such as superior quality or unique flavors, to justify higher prices.
3. **Adjust Strategically**:
   - Test initial prices, gather customer feedback, and refine as necessary. Flexibility helps cater to customer expectations while growing your business.

Avoid underpricing, which risks undervaluing your work, or overpricing, which may alienate potential customers. Your prices should reflect the time, effort, and craftsmanship poured into every product.

The Sweet Spot Between Passion and Profit

Running a bakery combines precision, creativity, and perseverance. By staying true to your vision, connecting with your audience, and delivering consistently high-quality baked goods, you can cultivate a successful business that brings joy to both you and your customers.

15

Baking with Kids

The Joy of Baking Together

Baking with children is a magical experience, filled with laughter, learning, and sensory exploration. It's a chance to bond while teaching essential skills, and the joy on a child's face as they see their creations come to life is unmatched.

Here are some tips for creating a fun and organized baking experience with young ones:

- **Preparation is Key**: Ensure every child has their own apron, a clean workspace, and the necessary tools within easy reach—rolling pins, bowls, and cookie cutters.
- **Hands-On Exploration**: Let children knead, roll, and shape soft dough. The tactile experience is not only thrilling but also helps them develop fine motor skills.
- **Encouragement and Independence**: Allow children to try tasks on their own, stepping in only when they need extra help. This builds confidence and a sense of achievement.
- **End with Fun and Teamwork**: When the cookies or breads are done and enjoyed, make cleanup part of the fun. Singing together while tidying up turns chores into cherished moments.

Shared baking projects create lasting memories, teaching kids that the kitchen is a place of creativity, warmth, and togetherness.

Simple and Fun Recipes for Kids

Start with basic recipes that are easy to follow and adapt. Here are some crowd-pleasers:

1. **Basic Bread Rolls**:
    - Ingredients: White flour, whole wheat flour, olive oil, milk, honey, yeast, and a pinch of salt.
    - Directions: Mix, knead, and let kids shape the dough into rolls. Bake until golden brown and enjoy with jam or cream.
2. **Decorative Sugar Cookies**:
    - Prepare simple sugar cookie dough and let children cut out shapes using cookie cutters. Once baked, provide sprinkles, edible glitter, and colored icing for decorating.

These recipes not only fill your home with delightful aromas but also give kids the joy of creating something from scratch.

Safety Guidelines

Keeping safety in mind ensures a stress-free experience for all:

- **Kitchen Cleanup**: Clean as you go to maintain an organized and enjoyable environment. Use downtime (like dough resting) to wipe counters and wash utensils.
- **Mixer Safety**:
    - Never let children place hands near mixers while in use.
    - Always turn off the mixer before removing ingredients from paddle attachments. Use a long-handled rubber spatula for this task.

Supervision and clear instructions help kids learn safe habits in the kitchen.

Teaching Baking Skills

Baking offers more than just treats—it instills valuable life skills:

- **Adaptability and Creativity**: Encourage children to try new ingredients or create their own designs for cookies and breads.
- **Patience and Precision**: Baking teaches the importance of following instructions, measuring accurately, and waiting for results.

Beyond home baking, these skills build a strong foundation for aspiring young chefs, providing a stepping stone toward mastery.

Conclusion

Baking, at its heart, is a celebration of creativity, community, and culture. It connects us to history, invites us to experiment with flavors and techniques, and provides moments of joy and togetherness—whether you're savoring a warm loaf fresh from the oven, decorating cookies with children, or sharing a beautifully crafted cake at a celebration. From mastering gluten-free adaptations to embracing the traditions of global baking, this journey of kneading, mixing, and shaping offers infinite opportunities to grow and innovate.

As you explore the rich tapestry of baking, remember that every crumb carries a story—of the ingredients you chose, the hands that shaped it, and the love poured into its creation. Baking is more than a skill; it's a way to express generosity, celebrate milestones, and bring comfort to everyday moments. No matter where you are in your baking journey, the magic lies not just in the finished product, but in the joy of creating something wonderful from humble beginnings.

So keep experimenting, learning, and sharing your creations. Whether you're baking for family, friends, or future customers, your passion is the key ingredient that turns every recipe into a masterpiece. Here's to many more delicious bakes and the happiness they bring!

www.ingramcontent.com/pod-product-compliance
Lightning Source LLC
LaVergne TN
LVHW092059060526
838201LV00047B/1466